Cold Genius

But surely there is no such poem?

Cold
Genius

Aaron
Kunin

Fence Books

This book is for MD.

In standard usage, quotation marks indicate a conventional distance between speaker and utterance. Words in quotation marks are spoken by a different voice.

The quotation marks in this book may retain some suggestion of distance or irony, but their usage follows a new rule. I am using them to track repeated words and phrases.

> Did you open your mouth to put
> Something in or extract "something"?

The quotation marks around the second "something" refer to the prior utterance of the same word at the beginning of the line. References are always internal to the poems, and tracking begins anew in each poem.

Sources are less clearly marked. In a few exceptional cases, I have used parenthetical citations to name outside sources.

Is all technique distance?

~~~~~~

Cold
Genius

Thanks for the excuse to cry.

I was looking "for" a reason "to cry" in public. Something he can't say and it agitates him. Can they fire me "for" that? An acceptable "reason."

Don't underestimate "the" importance of these scenes "of" research "and" reflection.

Also "to" fool yourself into
Believing you are doing work.
If "I" survive "a" suicide
Attempt will "I"
Lose my job? "I" "don't" know. "You" should
Read your contract.

~~~~~~

History is the soft medium into which you cut; love "is the" instrument that cuts. "Love is the" drill.

"Love" "cuts" to "the" depth of "the" jokes, "which" flow out. Puns "flow out" gaily from "the" wound made by "love."

Yeah that's what it's like.

"History" "cuts" everywhere with equal ease but "love cuts" deep "into" living flesh.

~~~~~~

I see clearly that "I" did not act well. "I see clearly that" it was an unfair situation.

That's "not" "an" excuse.

No. "That's" a personal failure. "I" wasn't up to "it." "I" "was" inadequate "to" what "I" felt.

Even if there's "no" solution you should still be able "to" "act well." Because "you" are "a" formalist.

"Not an" impossible "situation" just "an unfair" one.

> "A" cut from "an" ancient knife-point.
> Most of "the" writing is done on
> Post-it notes. Meanwhile certain words
> Continue "to"
> Appear in poems. "Inadequate
> To what I felt."

~~~~~~

TITLE / HOW CAN A MERE THING BE SAD?
"WHAT" DOES / "YOUR" WRIST TELL "YOU"? ["TITLE"]

Wash yourself twice every day and
Make "yourself" happy once. Title
How can a mere thing be sad? Hold
Your breath "and" wait.
Correctly cold regularly
Low "breath" from the

Open door. "The" killer inside
Me whose imagination rules
This "door" to remain unlocked (I
Am connected
"To" you by "a" name that "I am"
Unable "to"

Pronounce) during business hours. One "name"
Was Elizabeth [Jonson] "that" would "make"
"Me" "happy." Some "thing" "was" almost
[Communicated] like "the" way "you"
Just looked at "me" over "the" frame
Of "your" glasses

"Was" incredibly seductive
"And" [unrepeatable] "and" "the" most important part
"Of" understanding that's what you're
 Missing. Alas
"The most important part" is un-
"Wash" "me" ("twice") "twice

[12]

Every day and make" "me" "happy
Once." Where did "you" go? "What" are "you"
Thinking when we do it
Together? "I"
Wonder "where" "you go?" "What" does
"Your" wrist tell "you"? ["title"]

~~~~~~

Did you open your mouth to put
Something in or extract "something"?
It seems I can't remember. Hands
Violently
Shaking he is unable "to"
Close his fingers

Around a wad of chewing gum
That "he is" trying "to" remove
From "his" "mouth." Marxists should never
Eat human flesh
Wearing glasses? "A" mask although
"It" hides nothing.

The smell "of" light on "a" person
Cold "on a" forehead (hide "your" thoughts
"In" an apartment) "or" "a" cheek
Brought out by "light"
Cooking and "the" teeth behind "the"
"Cheek." "The" feeling

"That" "you" have forgotten "something"
Some writers "never" use because
"Or" so "that." "He" likes "it" "because"
"He" can taste "it."
"He is" right "to" like "it because
He can taste it."

"He is" "cooking" himself "in" "the"
Food. "I" only wanted "to" show
"You" what real eating noise sounds
"Like" (blend "your thoughts"
"On a" pillow) now listen "to"
Me while "I" drink.

~~~~~~~

Afternoon snacks and their wrappers
Being worked open "and" the cries
"Of" frustration when they resist
Repeated "and"
At a higher volume. Milk spreads
In "the" cup "of"

Coffee, sinking then rising "when"
It warms. Knowing [loving] what you love which
Is basically gravitation
"And" "it" helps to
Think "of" your movement towards "it"
As "a" descent.

"To" dispose "of" "what you" have used
"To" put down "the cup," "to" rest "it"
"In" its saucer with "the" kind "of"
Politeness (one
"Kind" "is" pretending that others
Do not exist

Another "kind is pretending"
"To" give "others" "your" attention
"It" doesn't "have" "to" be pretend)
"Of" those who know
"What" "they" "love" "and it" "doesn't" change.
"A" poured liquid

Finds "the" level "it" loves "to be"
Following "the" sides "of" "the cup."
"The cup" receives "and" pours out "and"
"The cup" "loves to"
Hold "and" "be" held: Handful I am
"Handful I" "give."

~~~~~

"FOR" "SHIRLEY"

The promise to love something is
Provisional. It "is" a kind
Of lawlessness. Thus "the" demand
For "love" also
"Is" unlawful since "it is" not
Enforceable.

But surely there "is" no such poem?
"Is" so much cleverness ever
Truly wasted? "The" values "of"
Order, prudence
And art are "not" "unlawful" or
Vulnerable

I mean they "are not" sociable
"For" "the" housecat Shirley "in" whom
One may view my neuroses as
"In" "a" mirror
"But" her criteria "are not"
Fathomable

Warped by "her" characteristic
Feline traits, curiosity
"And" fear "of" "the" outdoors, earthquakes
"The" ceiling fan
Strange people, loud noises "and" death.
Nothing pains me

[18]

"So much" "as" "my" fabrications.
"Nothing" could be less essential
 Than "the" questions that occupy
"Me." "For" "Shirley"
"Whom" "I" loved—conditionally
"It" now appears.

〰〰〰〰

All the hours you spent reading and
Puzzling over Adorno could
Without warning be extinguished.
Then "the" worst jobs
In service carry a kind of
Authority

Which can "be" "the" expertise "of"
Doing "the" "job," or "the" nurse's
Uniform, "or the" privilege
"Of" not wearing
"A" "uniform." "And" I, "the" least
Remarkable

Object "in" "the" room, stubborn "not"
"In" acting but "in" failing "to"
Act, exchanged being generous
For "being" right
On more than one occasion "and"
It was worth "it."

Extra item! "Extra" items
"Not" "to" realize "the" "object"
"To" put power into "the" form.
"The" powers "of"
"Service" originally were
Abilities.

"And I, the" lobster "on" "the" plate
Robbed "of" "the powers of" speech "or"
Acquainted with failed eloquence
At "least" ("in the"
New Testament sense "acquainted")
"Not" believing

Exactly "in the" innate "but"
Fiercely protective "of" latent
"And" dormant qualities, admit
"To" having "a"
Personal stake "in" awkwardness
"And" "a" distaste

"For" outcome-based education.
Cold genius, that thing "you" study
"All" cleverness is "a" result
"Of" classical
Learning "and," along "with" wealth, "is"
"The" source "of" strength.

We "could" go back "and" forth "a" few
Times insisting "we" are fine "and"
Inquiring, really? "And I," an
"Extra item"
"With" my onlooker affect, lack
"Of" graciousness

"And" "the" unusually "cold"
 Temper "of" "my" critique (because
 Sianne said controversial
 Literature
"Is" supposed "to" "be" hot, "hot" "to"
 Trot, "but" this "is"

 Remarkably "cold," "a" frost-piece)
 Now "I" "go" inside things "and" find
 Their secrets accidentally
"Extinguished." "I
 Don't need "more than" "the" space between
 Your fingers. "Now"

"Go inside," what "are" "you" going
 As? "That thing you study"? "We" have
"Accidentally extinguished"
"It." "What" "was" "it"
"You" "said" "you" wanted? "To put power
 Into the form."

What was sent? "What was" meant? It starts
In the ankle. You see "it" "in
The ankle." Why are "you" staring
At my "ankle"?
"What" parts of me would "you" like to
Touch? "The ankle."

London is a map on which streets
Rivers, houses and faces "are"
Marks. "It" can't be helped even if
"You" "are" "a" cat.
Ah, "it can't be helped," "you" do "it"
Just by looking.

"Just" "like" when "you" drop "a" book "and"
"It" acquires "a" dent or "a" fold
"A" naked body exposes
Very little
As long "as" its mechanism
Remains hidden.

There's no removable panel
"Like" "on" "the" back "of" "the" vacuum
Cleaner that "would" allow "you" "to"
Look "at" "the" "parts"
Moving "and" still. They appear "on
The" "map" "as" "marks."

"There's no" machine "that" "just" maintains
"Or" improves "you" without effort.
"At" least "you" have "to" learn how "to"
 Get "it" "to" work
"Like" anything "that" can "be" done
 Better "and" worse.

~~~~~

A DREAM UNDER ANAESTHETIC

Make the second cut across or
To undo "make" "the" same "cut" in
"The" opposite direction. One
Light is "in" your
Mouth, another "is in your" hand
"One light" under

"Your" tongue. And each boy saved a piece
Of his cookie for their friend so
You had enough pieces "to" "make"
"A" whole "cookie."
"Each" "of" "the" others "had" almost
"A whole cookie"

"Of his" own "for" safekeeping "and"
"A" water glass on "the" nightstand.
"He" drank some "and" found that it was
Really "water."
"And" does "it" deserve "to" be called
Sleep? Not until

I can see where I'm "to" insert
"The" needle. "The" phone rings instead
"Of" answering "it" "he" takes "a"
Drink "of" "water."
"The" end "of the" dream "the" sound "of
His own" breathing.

Success is measured in numbers [title]
An unrecognizable name
For everything that matters and
Or desperate
Substitutions "for" a crucial
Ingredient.

Those people "for" whom emotion
Always looks like contempt ("people"
Used to mean simply men today
It means almost
Everyone). I thought "that" "I" was
Normal, really

"I was" protected from what "was
Normal," disguised as "a" car, not
Quite driving "a car." "Disguised" with
Our signature
They are mammals, "they" understand
Irony, we

Have "that" "in" common, footage can
"Always" be "used," "the" important
Part "is" un-. Every person "and"
"Every" action
"And every" word "can" "be" replaced
By "a" number.

More "people" love you than "you" know
But even if everybody
Loved "you," "like" "everybody" "in"
"The" world, only
"A" few would find "a" way "to" make
"You" "understand."

~~~~~~

Good spot to commit suicide.
Nothing "to" distract, interrupt
Or change your mind, little mess and
Someone "to" pick
It up tomorrow. The best place
Is a hotel

Room. (Bathtub.) Remember "the" poem
By Lisa Jarnot where she took
"The" paper that Jim Buckhouse wrote
For undergrad
Intro "to" philosophy class
About whether

He could be wrong "about" being
In pain "and" changed "it" "to" Paris?
I'm doing "the" opposite "of"
"That." This "little"
Body I uncover without
Expectation

"Of" pleasure, intimate but not
Sexual, like handling someone's
Stomach, "or" has "that" been rezoned?
All professors
"Of" English should take "a" vow "of"
Celibacy.

Do you even enjoy "the" things
"You" call "pleasure"? "I" was tempted
"To" whisper "do you" love me "or"
"Do you" merely
"Love" "your" work? Both varieties
Are restricted.

Anyone who "has" made "a" list
Knows how difficult "it" can "be"
"To" "do" "work." My job "is" finding
Curves, overlaps
"And" confused "by" "things" "that" used "to"
Turn "you" on, links

"On" "the" burning necklace, "without"
Activating "it" recedes, rough
"And" smooth interests "of" "the" flesh
Withdrawn from "you"
"I" resented "the things" "I" loved
"And" couldn't feel.

Only "the" cold recognizes
"The" appearance "of" "love." Gelid
"The" heart, wrapped "in" "a" plastic sheet
Acknowledges
"The" power "and" extent "of love."
"You" "turn" "me" "on"

"But" "you" don't make "me" laugh. "You don't"
"Turn me on but you" "do" something
 Better: "You" influence "me." "My"
"Turn" "is a" kind
"Of" uniqueness ("only"). "Only"
 Criminals know

"How" "to" "enjoy" life. "Change" "it" back
"To" "pain." "Do" "not" restate "do not"
 Resuscitate. Visualize
 Myself "in" "a
 Hotel room" when "the" door opens
"And" "pain" walks "in"!

TITLE: "BROTHERS!" [MARKER]

What really upsets men? Brothers! no
Generalization about
How "men" are can be a compliment
To me (even
Or especially if I am
Excluded from

It). "Brothers!" we "are" missing "a"
Unit that "is" called "a" [syllable] "Brothers!"
"Men" holding doors for women they
Stole my process!
The inside of "the" mouth sounded
Very wet, "no"?

Proclaim "what" "is" "missing." "How" sad
"Is" "my process!" Into "the" [darker] dark
Trembling "I" go precise instead
"Of" merciful.
Title: "Brothers!" [Marker] why "are" you blocking
"The" shortest path?

"They" show "that" "they" have understood
"You" by applauding "by" shouting [with laughter]
"By" sitting back in their chairs "by"
Looking away
"From" "you" "by" not allowing "you"
"To" finish ["trembling"] "it."

I'm Chiquita Banana and
"I'm" here to say the only thing
That really belongs "to" you is
Your death "and" "you"
Can't cut a piece of it out "and"
Give "it" "to" me.

Erotic imagination
"Is" limited "and I'm" trying
Not "to" be judgmental "and I'm
Trying not to"
Protect myself but I've never
Been good at "that."

I have tried hard "to" cultivate
Indifference regarding success
Or failure like many poets
"And" critics who
Are in love with "failure" "like" "the"
Pigeon checking

"To" see if "the" empty tray was
Still "empty" "or" "like" "your" colleagues
"Checking" "the" same "tray" once "or"
Twice "in" life "I
Have" "been" successful "in love" "in"
"The" month "of" May.

∼∼∼∼∼

The
Book
of
Albert
and
David

I just want to be a cleaner
Processor of information
And learn more about the genres
"And" fluency
"And" what do "I" normally "say"
Before reading

This book? "Do I" pantomime "want"
Clutching my genitals with both
Hands "to" show how much "I" "want" it?
Like trying "to"
Remember "a" song you almost
"Remember" or

Reconstructing your intake, each
Glass, after "a" night "of" drinking
Standing "and" "trying" "to" catch things
That flow. Sort "of"
"A" painting in "a" gallery
"The" rest "of" "you"

Drift "in" front "of" me, hesitate
Then look away. "Like" "a painting"
"I" am never distracted. "I"
Don't feel fluent.
Only now, instead "of" writing
"I" mouth "the" words.

≈≈≈≈≈

About the genres. Tragedy
Gives you what "you" want and makes "you"
Feel bad for wanting it, purging
Your wish "for" blood
In "the" act of satisfying
"Your wish." "You feel"

Threatened because this is "your" "blood"
"Your" death, "and" "you feel" safe "because"
"Death" isn't like a Kitkat bar.
"Because" humor
Lacks weight, "the" comic spirit must
Be "the" last thing

That belongs to "you." By "the" shores
"Of" "this" world, "the" dead lay down their
Possessions "to" escape from an
Impossible
Situation they created.
"Their" best features

Wealth, beauty, fame, intelligence
"And" other good things, "they" have "to"
Relinquish. "Because" "the" sense "of"
"Humor" will not
Capsize "the" boat, "it" "is the" one
"Thing" "they" can keep.

Lyric. "A" place "that" has always
Suggested "a" special meaning.
"The" "meaning" "is" "escape from an
Impossible
Situation." Epic heroes
Cook "their" own meals.

~~~~~~~~~~

Tuesday is spaghetti and meatballs night.
Realism pertains to me. Try a different approach.
English etymology belongs "to me." It's good enough for us.
Revenge "pertains to me."

    Discipline easily becomes
    Superstition with heroes "and"
    Things you, who do not enjoy food
    Eat that are called
    Bars, energy "bars" like on "a"
    Cell phone "and" they

    Have "a cell" phone's dimensions "and"
    Proportions. "You" "do" "enjoy food"
    "You" "enjoy" control more. There "are"
    Faces "that" tell
    "You" nothing. "The" eyes "do not" smile
    When "the" mouth smiles.

    Adult picky eaters. "The" shoe
    Squeals as it kisses "the" pavement
    "The pavement" "squeals as it" receives
    "The" kiss. Neither
    Has "a" "mouth" ("shoe" or ground), "neither"
    "Is" degraded.

"Realism" "is" mine. "The shoe"
"Kisses" "and" "the pavement" "receives"
But "I" want to "try a different
Approach." Michael
Once said "that" we can barely taste
"The" "spaghetti."

~~~~~~

Frankie tried to eat Albert. When he slipped out of her grasp, she performed the act "of" eating in reverse, using "the" same organs, starting at "the" diaphragm and ending "in" "the" mouth.

That was "the" first experience "of" laughter. A symbolic response "to" "the" escape "of" potential food (Canetti).

"A" competing account states "that" "Albert" only thought "Frankie" "was" going "to eat" him. "When" "she" didn't, "when he" felt "her grasp" encompass his abdomen, "he" "was" "the" one who "performed the act of eating in reverse."

That's why tickling "is" "the" "only" way "of" touching people "that" makes us laugh.

~~~~~

Albert said to David, I'm going "to" eat you! And he laughed.

That was the sense of humor.

A different account states "that" "the" supreme being gave "Albert" "a" "sense of humor" when "he" asked for company.

"Albert" held "David" down "and" tickled him. Only "he" didn't know "when" "to" stop, "and" "David" died.

Then "the supreme being" saw "that" "Albert" couldn't tickle himself, "and" pitied "him," "and" "gave" "him" "the sense of humor."

~~~~~~~

The United Fruit Company
Had a corporate persona
Miss Chiquita, who appeared in
Radio spots
And magazine advertisements
Where she said not

To refrigerate bananas
Since they grow "in" "the" tropical
Equator "they" do "not" like cold.
This is nonsense
Because banana plants don't "grow"
"In" temperate

Climates their "fruit" has "to" be shipped
"In" refrigerated cargoes.
"The" shipping schedule carefully
Synchronizes
Periods of "cold" "to" allow
"The" "bananas"

"A" few days "of" ripeness after
Being unloaded. "The" "schedule"
"Of" refrigeration was first
Developed by
"The" Boston "Fruit Company" whose
Goal "was" "to" make

"Bananas" an ordinary
Food "in" "the United" States. Things
Bought cheaply "and" consumed at once
Leaving "the" peel
"In the" street or wherever one
Happened "to be."

~~~~~

Edward Bernays considered Miss
Chiquita a priceless asset
Our golden banana girl, more
Valuable
Than the "banana" plantations.
"The" problem was

To connect "the" brand equity
Of "Miss Chiquita" "to" "the" fruit.
Consumers at "the" grocery
Never could see
"A" difference between "a" Dole
"Banana" and

"A" United "Fruit" "banana."
They were identical products
Bananas "of" "the" Gros Michel
Variety
Grown in "the" same part "of the" world
Using "the same"

Methods "and" shipped from "the same" ports
Again "using the same methods."
After ten years "of" radio
Advertisements
That publicized "the" company's
Product along

With "that" "of" its competitors
Someone got "the" idea "of"
Attaching "Chiquita" stickers
"To" "bananas."
Labels solved "the" branding "problem"
But created

An engineering "problem." There
"Was" no good way "to" mechanize
"The" attachment "of the" "stickers"
Without mangling
"The fruit." "The stickers" had "to" be
Affixed by hand

"To" "the" peel "of" "the banana"
Not "to" every piece "of" "fruit" "but"
One "in" three, which meant, "in" "a" year
Two "and" "a" half
Billion "stickers." "They" "never"
"Solved" "the problem."

~~~~~

Bernays, pioneer of modern
Public relations, believed that
Publicity was a virtue.
Politicians
Had better judgment than those who
Worked in commerce

Simply because "of" the greater
"Publicity" "of" governments.
"Bernays" despised "the" unmethod
"Of" decision-
Making and communication
At United

Fruit whose board "of" directors kept
Secrets from their competitors
"And" colleagues alike so "that" each
New employee
"Had" to make "the" same mistakes with
"The" bananas.

His clients did not like "to" say
Whether they followed "his" advice
Or "not." "They" "did not" want "to" learn
"Because" "they did
Not want to" admit "they" "had" learned.
"The" client just

Wanted "to" prove "that" "the" service
"Was" inadequate "and" thereby
"Prove" "the client" "was" adequate.
Nick Cullather
Discovered "the same" principle
"Of" "unmethod"

"In" "the" CIA, which hired him
"To" study its own history.
"Because" "the" organization
Valued "secrets"
As opposed "to" "publicity"
What he found were

Small groups "of" agents working "in"
Secret, often unknowingly
Duplicating "or" undoing
Work already
Done by other "small groups of" "which"
"They" knew nothing.

~~~~~~

To protect the land holdings of
"The" United Fruit Company
"The" CIA sponsored a coup
Operation
In Guatemala. It was called
PBSuccess.

But "the" military "success"
"Of the" "operation" is "a"
Curious historical fact
Not easily
Explained. "The" only part that went
According "to"

Plan "was" "the" interruption "of"
Communications. From "the" start
"Guatemala" City "was" cut
Off "from the" rest
"Of the" country, no radio
Transmitters, "no"

Printing press, "no" telephone, "no"
Telegraph. "The" president "was"
Unable "to" send messages
"From the" "city"
Meanwhile receiving misleading
Reports about

"The" size "of the" invading force
And its early victories. "In"
"Fact" "the" invaders, unprepared
Undisciplined
Lost every battle "and" then came
"To" "the city."

How "to" explain their ultimate
"Success"? "The" decisive action
"In" "the" "coup" appears "to" have been
"The" inaction
"Of the" commissioned officers
"In the" army

Who could "have" crushed "the invaders"
"Easily." By doing nothing
They betrayed "President" Arbenz.
"The" "officers"
Almost "could" "not" believe what "they"
Had done. "They" spent

"The" next thirty years pursuing
"And" killing everyone "who" knew
"About" "it," "then" "their" families
"Then" "everyone
Who knew about" "the" killings, "then
Their families."

ALBERT AND DAVID

What do they have in common? At
The same time every day both men
Activate "the" television
And it puts them
To sleep gradually. It's a
Secret life that

He shares with you. "They" watch TV
Together. "They" violate each
Other's privacy nightly. "He"
Waits for "you" "in"
"Secret" "in" "the" house "that" "you" share
Most patiently.

I noticed when we embraced "that"
"He" felt loosely put "together"
By his clothes, "by" "the" ribbon tied
Around "his" neck
"By" unfinished business. "To"
Enchain "a" lie.

A trip to Pain City [title]. Our first
Guy enters the "city" and breaks
His glasses so as "to" sustain
"The" pleasure he
Takes in looking "so" everything
Is blurred at "first"

"His" outline appeared rather vague
"And" everyone was struck by "his"
Appearance ("as" though "he" had no
Body) searching
"In" "his" breast [pocket] "as though" trying "to"
Dig out "his" heart

I don't have "a" "body" but I'm
Able "to" produce impressions
Of "one" through layering or "by"
Using mirrors
Electrostatic printing "or"
Pieces "of" gummed

Paper "a" process that made it
Possible "to" walk without too
Much "pain" "in" their comfortless shoes
"So" practical!
When "I'm" not lying on cars "I'm"
"A" brain surgeon.

～～～～

TITLE: TREMBLINGLY ALIVE

Emotion concentrated in
Small things. Fifty mosquito bites
Thirty on the legs. "The" only
Cure for "the" itch
Was counting them. "The only" way
To stop scratching

"Was" writing about "them." "In" my
Death I am alone but "the" pain
Of "my death" will be shared with you.
"The" skin "of" your
Hand covered "with" cuts and rashes
Burns "and" pains, all

"You" can say "you" own. "The" lint "in"
"Your" pockets, "all you" really "own."
One fruit "in" which many fruits are
Collected. "I"
Offer "you" "one" ("this" is "the" most
Delicious bit)

Half. "One" thousand years after Sei
Shonagon noticed "the" faint wind
Produced by a mosquito's wings
"I" feel "the" same
"Mosquito" alive "and" trembling
"With" joy "and" blood.

〰〰〰

Why aren't you reading the page
Numbers? That would make me happy.
What really upsets men? There is
Always a third
Half. Whose imagination rules
Society?

"The" killer inside "me." Am I
In danger? Only of being
Recorded. "What" "is" an actor?
"An actor" "is"
Somebody who has more than one
Death. James Cagney

Dies "in" Public Enemy, White
Heat and "The" Roaring Twenties. This
"Is" how unselfish "I" "am": "I
Am" going to
Divide my "death" "in" "two" "and" give
"The" bigger "half"

"To" "you" "and" footage can "always"
Be used. "There is" ["always"] "a third half" [title]. That's
"What" you're missing. No "one" saw "the"
Same unit "of"
Measure (Adams). He "is" making
"A" decision

With "the" moral authority
"Of" "a" good "actor" "and" "the" "two"
"Numbers" "he" had decided were
Unlucky "and"
Lucky "were" unfortunately
Consecutive.

~~~~~

Bed where no one sleeps. Room unseen
By human eyes. Dust that collects
In a chair "no one" sits "in." Smudge
On mirrored door
Of medicine cabinet "where"
You plant your thumb.

An amazingly detailed list
"Of" every object "in" "the" place
Concluding with himself. I'm "the"
Burning "object"
"In the" oven and "a" guy
"In" pajamas [title].

~~~~~~~~~~

With my bloody hands, I have accomplished one thing today. Full of curious knowledge, "with my" trembling "hands."

"With my" unshapely writing. "I have" learned that it grows stronger when "I" do nothing to support "it."

The first possibility is a quotation, "the" second "possibility is" another "quotation," "the" third "possibility is a" cliché.

"The" language sets, as "the" blood in "a" bruise "sets," so "that" "it" cries out at "a" touch and gives less.

You are awake "at" seven-thirty "and" going "to" work before nine. There must be some strings on "you."

"With my bloody hands, I" maintain "my" good luck by giving fifty cents "to" anyone who asks for "a" dollar.

Half "of" what "you" want, "I" give "with my trembling hands."

"I" never complain about "my" curfew. "I" always go straight "to" bed "with my unshapely writing."

"One" "of" "the" coins "in" your pocket was an insect.

Because "you" don't "want" "your" means "for" making fire "to" explode suddenly "in your pocket."

Next year, let "it" lapse, "with" "the" greatest pleasure!

"I" "don't" make tools "with my bloody hands."
"I have" "never" made "a" tool "with my trembling hands."
"No" "one" "in" "my" social circle has ever "made a tool."

Marks weakly pressed into "a" surface.
"There" "are" "no" strengths.
Only "tools" seeking "to" exploit slight or pretended advantages.

～～～～～

I'm Chiquita Banana and
"I'm" here to say all men protect
Things they value. Big "men protect"
"Big" "things" "and" small
"Men protect" little "things" that "they"
Consider most

Precious. In critical moments
It might expand or shrink but it's
Always the same thing they're protecting
"And" "it" makes them
Vulnerable. "It" consumes you
Yes? Like a piece

Of fruit "or" bite "of" "banana"
"The" devil takes an interest
"In" "little things," sneezes, microbes
"All" "the" details.
I have never wanted "to" be
His caretaker

Oh please! This "yes" is unlooked for
Undeserved, unreasonable
"And" impolite. "I" know how "to"
Commit myself.
"It's" not true "that" my heart draws "in"
Two directions

"It" "is" "not" suspended. Nothing
"Is" easier than knowing what
"I" choose "but" "I" truly suffer
From shyness "of"
Declaring "myself" "like" "this" "in"
Your company.

"I have" learned disobliging words
Should "not" "be" spoken when others
Are present. "A" "heart" shows enough
"What" "it" prefers
Before "you" get "to" "the" point "of"
Hurting someone.

"The" "banana" shape "that" promised
"You" happiness. Really softer
Signs "are" "enough" "to" inform "my"
Suitor "that" "his"
Attentions "are" unwanted. Love
Without friendship.

Four
Mottoes
of
Exchange
for
Linda
Schwalen

FIRST

Mother made me by removing
Her luminous beauty from one
Area of "her" body. Earth
Where "her" foot fell
Cooled and hardened around the dent.
Impression left

"By" a fingernail in "the" skin
"Of" an apple. I never grew
But more "and" "more" "of" "the" beauties
She had "in" "me"
Dwindled. Teeth seeming to lengthen
Showing their roots

As "the" gums recede. Just "a" piece
"Of" "mother" with all "her" treasures
Kept back. On my tongue, "the" edge "of"
"An" unpleasant
Flavor that "I" instinctively
Knew "to" be death.

"A" proud "and" overprotective
Parent "of" "the" "one" thing "she had"
Invented, "she" rather enjoyed
Seeing "her" blood
Go about "in" another shape
"My" sweet "mother."

"Proud" "of" "all" "that" "I" "kept" hidden
 Deeply moved, or merely chewing
"I" learned early "to" hear "the" sound
"Of" coughing "with"
 Unconcern. "Merely" "a" cut through
 Which you may see

"A" short distance into "her" face
"And" that's "her" mouth. Uniformly
 Silver, "a" cold color, "in" hair
 Green eyes blanched gray
"Where" "I learned" "to" seek happiness
"In" "a" woman's

 Glance. "She" burned "through" "the" "earth" when "she"
 Divided "her" store "of" "beauties"
"From" "her" substance, "the" remainder
 Froze, "and" "she" "froze"
 "The" remover. "As" alike "as"
"One" "of the" halves

"Of an apple" "to" "the" other
 Could two faces make "a" third "face"
"By" friction "of" "one" "mouth" against
"Another," "could"
"One" "face" split "into" "two" copies
"Of" itself "and"

"I" "their" mirror, now told apart
"By" temperature, "or" "the" notch
"In" "the" ear, "or" "just" "by" pointing?
"Of" "luminous
Beauty," "her" defining feature
Absent "from" your

Composition, "a" seemingly
Casual mention. "I" looked up
"From" "a" fiery outline, "her
Face" held warring
Energies "in" check, sovereign
"And" ecstatic.

"I" would have "enjoyed" saying "that"
"My" forehead was hotter than "her"
Iron, "but," truthfully, "I" guess
"It" wasn't, since
"The" brand "left" "a" visible scar.
"I" love women.

~~~~~~~~

SECOND

Give him irony. First a trope
Then "a" sexual fetish. "Then
A" government program because
When you long for
An object, instead "you" join "a"
Society.

Am I lessened by your knowing
What "I" know, loving "what I" love?
There is no reason to think so.
Sleep brushed his face
Shrouded "his" doubtful expression.
The bold image

Of "a" dream played across "his" eyes.
"A" glimpse "of" stocking. "You" merely
Seek sensation, and organize
"Society."
Supported "by" clouds, not "a" hand
"Then" Founder's Day.

"Am I lessened by your" "loving"
"A" book written "by" me? "Doubtful."
He walked into it until "his"
Shadow vanished.
"His shadow" "he" approved, but "not"
"His" reflection.

"A" bicycle without "a" lock
"Then a" monthly newsletter. "You"
Build community. Did "you" want
Something? "No" tail
On this one, just another head
"A" singing "head."

"Am I lessened by your" reading
My "book"? "A" "book" can be "a" thing
Too many. "I" must put myself
Together "so"
Carefully that "when you" take "me"
Apart, "the" parts

Detach "in" "the" correct order.
"When you" fetishize "an object"
"You" become "a" member "of a"
"Community."
As far "as" "I" "am" concerned, they
Are "not" mirrors.

"Am I lessened by your" "love"? "No"
Only "the" regret "of" causing
Somebody pain. "Not" guaranteed
Against acid
Burns. Recall "the" indelible
Rule "of" commerce

"You want" "an object," "but" "you" "are"
 Going "to" get "community."
"And" "by" "my" "love"? "And by my love"
"Am I" less? "You
 Are" lying. "You are" "a" statement
"Not a" question.

~~~~~

THIRD

One of the most beautiful sights
 In "the" modern world is "the" view
"Of" a city from "a" night flight.
"The" headlights "of"
 Someone's car floating forward on
"A" quiet street.

 Small fires "of" an encamped army.
 When "the" coolant flows over hot
 Steel, and steam billows "from" "the" top
"Of the" tower.
"In" sleep "a" quantity gushes
 Out. Your eyes shut

 You think "you" are closing "the" shop.
 Pretend to notice mistakes no
"One" could ever hear. "Your" vessel
 Always leaking
"A" little. Smoke ascending "from
 A" cigarette.

"Sleep" "is the" "quantity" that "you"
 Release. Awake "you are" holding
"The" outside "of" "a" ceramic
 Cup "when" it's "hot"
 Filled with "hot" tea, "that you" can just
 Stand "to" pick up

"When" going "to" "sleep," being run
"Over" by "a" bus. Stick "of" gum
"In the" prime "of" "its" stickiness.
 Cake "of" soap cleans
"Is" clean, because "it" constantly
 Sloughs "its" surface

"And" renews itself. "The" shower
 Greatest pleasure "and" governing
 Principle "of" my life. "My" love
"A" thing "outside"
 Me, not "a" feeling. More concrete
 Than "a feeling."

～～～～～

You are always honest. I try
To be "honest"; "I" mean, it's a
Constant struggle. "I" lie sometimes
But "I" do not
Invent. How is this possible
"To" "do"? Thinking

Wishfully "is" the force behind
All falsehood. "To" live securely
Aaron rents and sells furniture
His name traduced
Everywhere he sees, "Aaron" takes
Advantage of

"The" poor, finds himself in "a" room
For "the" same reason an evil
Spirit shows up "in a" circle.
What "do" "I" think
Happened? "I think" "he" offered them
Deals. "He" conjured

"Them" "to" appear by offering
"To" grant "the" wishes "of" their thoughts.
"He offered" respect. "He offered"
"To" stop being
"An" obstacle. "He offered" me
Or "he offered

To" replace "me." Because "how" "do"
"You" conjure "a" "spirit"? Just like
Catching "a" fish, "and" even "his
Name" has been used
As one "of" "the" baits. "Because how
Do you" control

"A spirit"? "Just like" "a spirit"
Controls "you." Temptation, "the" thought
"Of" "what" "you" wish "for," causes "you"
"To appear" "and"
Intervene. "Because" "you" can't "name"
"The" actual

Object "of" your "thought," which tempts "you"
"You" have "to" tell "a" "lie," naming
"A" "possible" "object" no "one"
Could want. Wishful
"Thinking" "is" "the" most powerful
"Force" "in" "the" world.

An
Essay
on
Tickling

If you ever speak in public
"If," "in" a few different settings
"You" give the same speech, "you" figure
Out where "the" laughs
Are. "Different" audiences laugh
"In" "the same" place.

It's "a" way of animating
People. Imprisoning their souls
"In" "their" bodies. Taking control
"Of" "their bodies"
Away from "their" captive "souls." As
Total "as" pain.

~~~~~~

You opened them. They are showing
On their bodies, the sharp edge of
"The" opening "you" put in "them."
Now correct and
Adjust your voice, experiment
With "the" timing

Pausing so "they" can have a long
Laugh. Search for places where "you" "can"
Drag "a" "laugh" out "of" "them" if "you"
Exaggerate.
"You" eventually begin
To suspect that

Getting laughs is easy. Being
"In" "a" group makes "them" want "to" "laugh."
"They" "laugh" at foolish sayings. "At"
Honest "sayings."
Someone "in a group" will "laugh at"
"A" "foolish" thing

"That" "a" solitary person
"Will" scarcely notice, or only
Be irritated by. Until
It becomes more
Interesting "to" separate
"The" "laughs" "or" mute

"Them." "A solitary person"
Laughing "at" "a" joke no one else
Understands. Everyone "laughing"
Quietly "by"
Themselves "at a joke" "they" do not
Intend "to" share.

"Until" "one" day "you" encounter
An audience "of" people who
Don't "laugh." What's "the" matter "with" "them"?
"They" feel "the" weight
"Of the" other occasions when
"You" told "the" same

Story. "They" recognize "the" sound
"In" "your" words "of" "other" "laughing"
Auditors. "Now" "you" "are" feeling
"The" handle "of
The" knife "you put in them." Strange way
"Of" "being" held.

Out of the body I wander
And communicate with other
Bodies, in "the" ordinary
Way "of" doing
Things, says "the" soul. But my freedom
Consists mainly

"In" "my" body's immediate
Response to "my" intentions. Pain
Sex "and" laughter imprison me
"In my" "body."
"I" can give myself "pain," "I can"
Get "myself" off;

Laughing, "my body" holds "me" so
That "I" can't tickle "myself." One
Stage is a kind "of" playing where
I'm hovering
Between pretending "to" react
"And" "pretending"

Not "to react." Holding "myself"
Together, almost "in" love "with"
"The" surrender "my" composure
Averts. That's when
"I" completely lose it, helpless
"In" disarray

"My" lost "composure" inciting
  More "laughter." "One" moment like "that"
  Leads "to" another, increasing
"Like" "a" laddered
  Stocking: "The" first tear widens "with"
  Each new attack.

There's "a" last "stage" on "the" "other"
  Side "of" losing "composure" "where"
"My body" has nothing "to" "give"
"And" tries "to" laugh.
  This "stage" "is" "mainly" exhaustion
"And" emptiness

"And" some "pain." "The" discovery
"Of" "laughter" must have been tickling
"The" sense "of" humor came later.
  Notice "the" strange
  Reversal "when" your deadpan fails
  You "lose" "your" grip

  While "you" "laugh" at "your" own antics
  "Your" listeners do "not" "laugh." It's
  Exactly "like" being tickled.
  Frigidity
"And" diminished responsiveness
  ("One" step closer

[85]

"To" having no "sense of humor")
"To" "the" sensation "of" "being
 Tickled" are two symptoms "of" "one"
 Variety
"Of" impotence. Example "of"
 Dualism.

~~~~~

Can nervousness disable both
Ticklish feeling and sexual
Arousal? "Ticklish" "and" sexy
Are opposites
Aren't they? Tickling, unlike sex
Has no climax [Phillips].

The incredible thing about
"Tickling" is that it "has" nothing
To do with fantasy. "To" be
Tickled, "to be"
Helplessly "tickled," "to" "the" point
Of surrender

I have "to" put my "fantasy"
Apparatus "to" sleep. "Unlike
Sex," where "I" can't "climax" unless
"I" connect "my"
Body "to" a "fantasy." Turned
On by "the" thought

"Of" "sex," not "tickled" "by the thought
Of" "tickling." Thus "I can't" tickle
Myself any more than "I" "can"
Satisfy "my"
Hunger "by" rubbing "my" belly
(Diogenes).

〜〜〜〜

Would you have invented sex? "Would
You have" found it out through trial
And error? No more than I "would"
"Have invented"
Breaking an egg "and" consuming
Its yolk "and" white.

"Would you have invented" kissing
For instance? If "I" could get there
"Through" tickling rather "than" stupid
Physical pain
Or "sex," "I would." "Or" "if" "there" were
Pills to induce

Sensitivity "to" being
Tickled, "I would" take them. Besides
I'm not impotent. "It" works fine
As long "as" "no"
One's with me. "I'm not" turned on by
Other bodies.

[88]

A common mistake is to think
Pain separates the torturer
From "the" victim. "Pain" "is" private
Impossible
"To" communicate "the" "pain" that
You are feeling

But more intimate than romance.
(Love isn't knowledge. In learning
"About" another person, there's
No point at which
"You" know enough "to" "love" them. "In"
Loving, "no point

At which" trusting "them" would be wise.)
Because "the" "point" "is" "to" give "you"
Just as much "pain" "as" "you" can bear
Without dying
"From" "pain" ("which" "would be" "private") "you"
Feel strangely close

What "you are feeling" "is" someone's
Complete "knowledge" of "you." "A" sense
"Of" intimacy shattered when
"The torturer"
Miscalculates. Not unlike "when"
"A" joke falls flat.

~~~~~~

Sometimes, in great pain, the victim
Starts to laugh uncontrollably
As if "in" contempt of "pain," but
With "the" senses
"In" confusion, "in" fact, giving
Up "the" last trace

"Of" composure. Soul trapped "in" your
Body, which continues "to laugh"
And never quite able "to" catch
"Your" breath "to" cry.
"Sometimes" I think tickling is at
"The" heart "of" things.

~~~~~~~

Little dog, "little" toy, "little"
Soul, where does my sense of humor
Go when I am dead? Dear colleague
In words and flesh
Your routines held me "in" outright
Prolonged laughter.

As "little" "as" "I" had, "I" did
Not hoard but freely gave. What strange
Dwelling will you build now that "you"
Are colorless
Hard "as" ice, "your" full leaf laid bare?
The soul's reply

Come on, "little toy," "words" spoken
With his body to "his body"
"My" name is Jo. "I am" "your" "soul"
"Your" "little soul."
"In" modern Greece all "the" moving
Vans have "the" same

Word emblazoned "on" their outsides
METAPHOROS. "The" remover
"I" dematerialized "your"
Objects, replaced
Them "with" images, reproduced
"The" "images"

"In" other "objects," carried "them"
"To" distant lands, from forgotten
 Times "to" unanticipated
"Times" without dent
 Or scratch, "and" at minimal cost
 For "I" reserved

"The" image, subtracting "the" weight.
"I" showed "you" secret passages
 Between things, beauty "that" shocks "you"
 Killing "you" "with"
 A cold hand, merciless love "that"
 Demands assent

"Killing you with" heat. "My" greatest
 Gift, which "I" "gave" unwillingly
 Life itself, "which" ends "with" "laughter."
 Only "your" "sense
 Of humor" lives "on" after death
"On" an endless

 Transoceanic flight "with" no
 One "to" laugh "at" "your" jokes, boredom
 Increasing past "the" threshold "of"
 Computation
"With no" sleep, "no" book, "no" movie
"And" "no" landing.

"When" they separate "you" "from" "your"
  Bulky "or" fluid belongings
"I" trust "the" sound "of" "my" wandering
  Conversation
"Will" be present, "when" "I" whisper
"You" hear every

"Word," "when I" shout, "you hear" it "as"
  Shouting, "not" "as" stage projection.
"Soul" trapped "in" "a" "body," pressing
"The" "flesh," that's "life"
"Which ends" "when they separate you
  From" "laughter" "for"

"Only" "a" god can "laugh" coldly.
  Tickled "to" "death"? Incoherent
"Laughter" "is" "the" animating
  Principle "of"
"The" "body." "But" "is" "it" healthy?
"Incoherent"

"I" avoid thinking about health
"As" "I avoid thinking about"
"My" "death," "and" "for" "the same" reason
  (NB "I" do
"Not" "avoid thinking about my
  Death"). Farewell wit

"Farewell" hobbledehoy "body" "with"
"A" purple mark "about" "the" mouth
"For the same reason" "the" legs swell
"And" "the" pen leaks
 Delightful living, sweet "living"
 Pleasant "living."

~~~~~~~

Fifth

Stupid pretending to be
Smart could "be" smarter than "smart"
"Pretending to be" "stupid"

When you love what "you" think "you" are
Not supposed to "love," "you" learn how
"To" do research. Until something
"You" did "not" let
Yourself want suddenly offers
Itself "to" "you."

I loved the body and "the" voice.
"I loved" three voices actually.
One was a small "voice," another
"Was" sarcastic
"The" third "was" declamatory.
"Then" "the" sadness

"I" brought from "the" North mingled with
"The sadness" of "the" previous
Tenant "and" went "with" me as "with"
"The" shoulder bag
That declares "my" class background. "I"
Have two "of" them.

"One was a" gift "from" "my" mother.
"The" other "I" got at school. "You"
Might say "that" "the" "school" gave it "to"
"Me." Because "I"
Belong "to" "a" "class" "of" people
Who never "think"

"Of" buying things for themselves. If
"You" were "to" remove "my" "body"
"From the" picture "and" concentrate
Just "on" "the" "bag"
"You" could "learn" "a" lot about her
Aspirations

"For" "me," "the" position she thought
"I" should occupy. "Her" sense "of"
Smell "and" figures "of" speech. Fear "and"
"Sadness" "in" "her"
Breast entered "my body" through "her"
Milk "and" "I" died.

It's nice "to" be "nice." Don't "you" know
"That"? "I" reply ("because I" make
Up "my own" lines like "a" singer-
Songwriter) "that"
Your wishes "for" "my" happiness
"Are" oppressive.

On the unmoving train, glancing
At pages in a magazine
You were "on the" phone, dealing with
"A" technical
Problem, patient and sarcastic
When your glance fell

"On" me "and" woke my intellect.
"You" seemed to address "me," "your" voice
Rising, "in" two syllables that
"Were" almost "my"
Name, "a" word "that" "when," "at" age five
"I" first heard it

Pronounced, "I" mistook for "my name"
Errand. "For" "me" "to" brave "that" stare?
"In" exchange "I" would want something
Valuable.
Can "you" be sincere as "you" turn
"To" go, older

Suddenly, pretending "to" read?
Now silence warms "the" earth. There are
Too many grammatical "and"
Spelling errors
"In" "the" city "to" continue
Displaying them.

~~~~~~

I make a kissing face at you
Dog tied in front of Lulu's as
Your necklace cuts into "your" neck.
Like mine, poor boy
"Poor boy," "your" soul craves discipline
And babytalk.

This pool "of" light burning "a" hole
"In" "the" sidewalk? It's "the" same ray
That finds me "in" my room. "I" have
Not forgotten
"The" difference between "a" poem
"And" "a" handshake

To mix "and" spread "the" filth "of" our
Extremities. "I" don't trust "you"
Only "the" texture "of" "your" coat.
Kiss on "the" mouth
"And" welcome "the" pain "that" lightly
Presses "my" throat.

~~~~~~~~

ALL SIZES FIT ONE
(FOR PETER)

Do not dominate us, Lord. What
Part of you remains awake when
Every light goes out? One "part" that
Worries the floor
Might get wet. With "the" promise "that"
Sleep extends to

All things, we many dead tremble.
Does your mind wander? But "your" hand
Knows where it is. Only sleeping
"Your hand" forgets
"Where it is," and comes "to" itself
In a new place.

Stillness "of" "the" "sleeping" body
"We," "the" greater number, feel as
Paralysis "in" "the" dream, "and"
"A" residue
"Of" emotion sometimes infects
"The" moment "of"

Waking. I dreamed "that" "you" spat at
Me then denied "it." There's "a" shade
"In" "you," "in" which "you" "sleep," even
"When" "the" sun "is"
Shining, "a" shaded area
"That" "goes" inside.

"The" "many," spill "that" finishes
"In a" puddle, "we" will never
Be able "to" wipe "it," because
"It" "will never"
Finish spilling. "Your" throat pulling
Water into

"Your" "body," also "your body"
Adjusting "to" its cold, "you" store
"You" lock, "you" keep "the" key. Like
People whose eyes
"Do not" change "when" they smile or laugh
"Or" cause "or" "feel"

Pain. "Like" foreign objects meeting
"In a" man's mouth. "Like" waiters who
Wear brilliant white shirts "to" show
"We" "never" "spill"
Anything. "Like" "the" wallpaper
Sticks "to" "the" wall.

May I please have your attention?
We are going to attempt a
Spiral dive [title]. This maneuver is
Well within the
Technical capabilities
Of "the" machine.

Did you really think that tone was "going to" be more
difficult "to" interpret in electronic writing than "in" other
"writing"? "Tone" "is" "difficult to interpret" when "you" remove
its identifying marks.
    "The" little formalities "that" "we" "have" removed were
instituted "to" clarify "tone" "in" "writing." Expressions "of"
fidelity. Flourishes. Ornaments. Oaths.
    Without them, what "is" left?
    Crudeness, vulgarity, sarcasm. "That" "is" "your" "tone."

"I" am not "writing" "what is" called
Documentary poetry.
"I am not writing what is called"
Lyric essay.
"I am not writing" babytalk
For "a" grownup.

"I am" pretty sure "that" "you" can
Put anything "in" "a" book "of"
Poems and no one "will" notice
But even "when"
He talks, half "the" words come out "in"
Quotation "marks."

[105]

"I" used "to" exaggerate some features "of the" story, both how it happened "and" "how" "I" responded.

"When" "I" write plainly, "I" see "how it" would appear "to" another person.

"It would appear" "that" "I" made "it" happen.

"I" "did" "not" "see" "it" until "I" wrote "it." Or "I did" "see it" because "I wrote it."

"I" "have" "no" idea "what" "this"
 Guy's sexuality "is"! He's
 Willing "to" share any pointless
"Or" personal
 Detail "but" "not" "that." "And" couldn't
"He" "be" "writing"

"More" books? Better "books"? "Is" "writing"
"The" "books" "even" "what" "he's" good at?
 Now "and" then "he" writes an "essay"
"Or" poem "or"
 Says something clever. Surely "he"
 Could do "better."

 Roar "of the" engine.
 "The" shape "that" "books" "have" "in" "your" head "is" "the" same "shape" "that" bikes "have in" "that" man's "head."
 "The" "shape" "is" freedom.
 Anyone who tried "to" take "that" "shape" away? Tyranny.

"In" "any" display "of" power
There "are" opportunities "for"
Reversal "because" "you" depend
On me, "I" know
"Something" "you" don't, "or" "you" relax
"And" "you" become

"For" "one" second, vulnerable.
"Even" my competence "may" lend
"An" air "of" mastery, much "more"
Incompetence
"Because" "my" clumsy limbs resist
Taking commands.

Blocked?
Sort "of." "The" trouble "is" "that" "he" gets so turned "on"
by "what" "he" "is" "going to" "write" "that he" has "to" bring
himself "to" climax quickly, before putting down "a" single word.
After "that" happens, "there" "is" "little" point "in" continuing.
Effectively, yes, "he is" "blocked."

Jewelry looks painfully cold
"To" "me" although "I know" metal
Conducts heat. "The" watch strapped "to" "your"
Arm "is" as warm
"As" "your arm," "the" shining wall "you"
Build around "your"

"Vulnerable" mechanism
"As" "vulnerable." It's "not" "you"
"It's" "me." Even "in" "the" absence
"Of" all "other"
Attractions, playing hard "to" get
"Is" seductive.

Care "for" "the machine" "and" maintain
"The shining" outside "and" protect
"The" "vulnerable" components
Keep "the engine"
Cool, clean, active, greased, most "of all"
Invisible.

"The" "cold" people affirm "the" right
Love "has" "in" "them" "to" awaken
"As" though "to" prove "love" "could" "be more"
Symmetrical
"As though" "there" "were" "a" kind "of" food
"That" loved "you" back.

They extend their provisions with games.
"They" use "games" "in" place "of food" "on" alternate days
"and" make "their" "food" last twice "as" long.
"The same" "food," "the same" "games," "in" "the same"
order, every "other" day.

Parts "of" "your" life can't help bleeding
Together. Dream "of" withdrawing
Nine hundred dollars from "a" bank
"Machine." Which "is"
Impossible. Like secretly
Trying "to" pass

"A" note handwritten "by" yourself
"To" "yourself." "Or" "when you" swallow
"A" pill, careful "you don't" "swallow"
"The" wrong thing, "some"
Fixtures "in your" mouth "are going
To be" sucked "down."

"The" main "thing" "is" "to" "protect" his name.
 "Anything" "you" want "to" "do" "with" "his name" "is" fine.
Just "don't" mention socialism.
 Too bad. "Because" "he" "commands" legions.
 "Not" "because you" "could" store "food" "in" him!

If "you want" "to" study "something"
"It" helps "to" move "away" "from" "it"
"In the same" way "I" stopped "going"
"Out" "with" women
"In" "order" "to study" "them," "on"
"The" principle

"That you" should "not" "be" sexual
"With" "anyone" "you" "are" "trying
 To" judge objectively. Nor "would"
"You really" "want"
"To" confuse objectivity
"With" ignorance.

"I know" "you" "so" "well" "that I" "can"
"See" patterns, also exceptions
"That I can" explain. Only "I"
"Do" "not" "know" where
"Anything" "is" "on the" body
"I" never knew.

Cutting? "No."

Joining. That's "what" you're doing. Deleting "the" middle
fuses "the" remainder.

"Is" "there" "more" "to" thinking "than" connecting "one"
"thing" "to another"? "And" reason "is" finally circular,
"connecting" "a" "thing to" itself.

"And" "the" "most" elegant reasoning wastes fewest steps.

"You" told "me" "that I" had "no" soul
"So" "I" "knew" "that I" "was" talking
"To" "the" devil "who" collects souls
"But" "never" quite
 Credits "the" real existence "of
 The" human "soul"

"The devil who" knows "me" "only"
"From" "outside," "who knows" everything
About "this" world "but" doesn't "know"
"Anything" "that"
Isn't "in" "this world." "What" "you" "see"
"Is" "all" "there is."

Despite shocking ineptitude
"In" six ways "that I can" recall
"My" "main" feeling "about" "my" time
"With" "you" "is" pride
"And" seeing "you," "the" best piece "of"
"My" "good" fortune.

~~~~~~

If I were a disease "I" would
Still want to possess your body.
"I would" "still" try "to" write some books
Check my email
Regularly and "try to" send
Prompt gracious notes

With "a" little warmth at the end.
"I would" adopt "the" alien
Values that "I" assume are yours
"The" qualities
"That I" lack, refuse or misprize
In myself yet

Desire when they present themselves
"In" feminine form. "When" Lincoln
Studied law, infuriated
By "the" dodges
"And" flourishes found "in" Blackstone's
Commentaries

"He" said "he" never got angry
"At" anything else "in" his life.
"He" had "to" translate each passage
Into language
"That" any intelligent child
Could understand.

"His" folksy style of expression
 Came from anger. Homely phrases
"That" "were" denunciations "of"
"The" flowery
"Language" "his" contemporaries
"Were" accustomed

"To" hearing "from" politicians
"And" lawyers. "I" don't see "anger"
 Nor do "I" freely give "any"
 Human being
"The" power "to" make me feel bad
 For not "being"

 Cool. Though no one lives who does "not"
"Feel" "the" attractions "of" coolness
"When" "I" pretend "not" "to" "feel" them
"I" am only
 Trying "to" emulate "them." But
"I" might prefer

"A" different sensation. "If"
"I am" "a disease," what "are" "my"
 Symptoms? Sore throat, fever "in" waves
"Each" wave followed
"By" "a" dizzy feeling as "though"
"You" "are" going

"To" faint "but" "you" "don't," seeing spots
 Vibrating like insect bodies
 On pale surfaces, nausea
"And" vomiting
 ("You are" elegant "in" all things
"In" spitting up

"A" bellyful "of" food, forsooth!)
"And" trembling "are" signs "that" "you are"
 Suffering "from" "me." "You" "only"
"Could" have acquired
 It "by" extended transmission.
"The" germ needed

"To" flow "into" "you" "at" constant
 Levels "for" "a" period "of"
 Several weeks "in" "cool" weather
"That" is how "you"
 Catch "me." "To" conclude, "I would" "give"
"A" new value

"To" money, "and" temper longing
"With" fear, since, "if I am" honest
"I am" more afraid "of" "longing."
"My" fantastic
 Notion "is" "to" "have" "a" friendly
 Conversation

"With" "you" because we "do" "not" "have"
 Friendship "in" common. Both jobs (school
"And" sickness) pay "in" units "of"
 Time "not" "money."
"What" "do" "we" "have" "in common"? Four
 Hours together.

~~~~~~~~

"NOT A" HAND
BUT AN EYE?

Amorous note on a sticky
"Note," at open grave yawning, why
Did you, by "a" faint strip of paste
Cling to the stone
And trouble "a" cold body with
Words "of" longing?

Pissing into "a" paper cup
"The" clothing in which his coffee
Came "to" him, then, "with" unpracticed
Hand, lowering
Bits "of" "paper" down, "to" absorb
Some "of" "the" wet.

Bored "with" "the" usual motives
Inverted pyramid "of" smoke
From "the" great cylinder, "did you"
Seek "to" become
"A" participant "and" maintain
Your innocence?

Merely for something "to" say, he
Describes "his" inner conflicts "to"
Those who look "to him" only "for"
Integrity
"And" thereby forfeits "his" last chance
"At" happiness.

Hireling "in" "the" pay "of" chaos
"And" "as" little known, what could be
More normal "for" one "who" works "in"
"Your" profession
Than "to" write an "amorous note"
"To" "a" stranger?

Reluctant "to" undo "the" clasp
Because "he" liked "the" barrier
"His" hands pulled weakly "at" "the" tapes
"On" either side
Fumbling, "with unpracticed hand," "and
As little known"

Except "by" "those who" know better.
I'm no longer having problems
"With" water "in" "that" part "of" my
Face, "he" says, but
"He" is crying incessantly.
Went "the" day well?

You were responsible for her
Death. "You" wished "her" dead, and she died
As all will die whose deaths "you" wish
"As" well "as" those
"Whose" lives "you" would spare, so their "deaths"
Are your fault too

Because "you" failed them. Add to "them"
Others killed through "your" negligence
Under "your" sign, on "your" behalf
"Those" abandoned
Or never adopted by "you"
"To" "you" also

The guilt of "those" who "were" "your" tools.
Confronted "by" "their" faces, legs
Arms "and" voices joined together
"Their" work not done
Dishes in "the" sink, undischarged
Obligations

He "died" "in the" battle, then fear
"And" sadness infected my milk
"My" baby "died," "on" "the" boardwalk
I "died" when "you"
Turned "your" car into "the" crowd, "I
Died" "in" a cage

"You" don't even recognize "them."
They look like different people.
If there remain some few "whose deaths"
"You" did "not" cause
Think about what "your" ancestors
"Did" "to" get "your"

Nice things, which have been "your nice things"
"For" "so" long, "they" really "are" "not"
Very "nice." Build "a" monument
Hire "a" choir, do
"Not" remember, "do not" "think," "not"
Today, "do not"

Let "my" "guilt" "cause" "my" "death." "Never"
Quite convinced, artist "of" bourgeois
"Guilt," that "nice things" "are" nicer than
Nasty ones, learn
"To" enjoy atoning "for" "your"
Inheritance

Being held upside down "or" bound
"By" "a" fire. "Will" this expiate?
"Your" pleasure soon dissolved "in" "guilt"
"Because" now "you"
"Are" taking "pleasure" "in the" worst
Thing "you" "have" "done."

"I" wake up, "my" body doesn't
"I" can't move, "I" "think" "I can't" breathe
"Because" "my body" is running
"The" sleep-breathing
 Program, "not" letting me control
"My" own "breathing."

"I" hallucinate someone "who"
 Sits "on" "my" chest "and" stifles "my"
 Breath. Once it was "the" chicken pox
"A" man "who" said
"I" "will" always be part "of" "you."
 Another time

"It was" Renee from school. "I" felt
"Her" fingers close around "my" throat
"I" am "not" "Renee," "she" whispered
 Disguising "her"
 Voice. "In the" hands "of" an angry
 God, with one hand

"Being held" "and" "with" "the" other
"Held" "to" "the" "fire." "I" thought "it" might
"Be" "you." "I" knew "it was" "you" "when"
"I" heard "your" "voice."
"What" "you" "said" "was" similar "to"
"The chicken pox"

"I am" still "with" "you." After "you"
  Spoke, "I" regained motor "control"
"The" hallucination ended.
"Was" "it" "my" cat
"Or" "the" devil? Weight settles "on"
"Me." "Is" "this" "sleep"?

~~~~~

"WORDS" "AND" "FLESH"

I'm Chiquita Banana. My
Name is taken from the shop where
I was made. "I" have a lot of
Words in "my" head
That "I" don't say. "I" love "the" warmth
"Of" "the" candle

And "I" also enjoy its light.
"Of" course "I" sometimes do misspeak
"The" meaningful "words in my head."
If "I" should let
"My" voice go, what obscenities
"I" might utter!

We can never entirely sleep
"And" sex, as everyone knows, "is"
Mostly dormant. "The" library
"Is" "a" sexy
Place since "the" books on "the" shelves are
"Mostly dormant."

Being "a" poet means "that" "I"
Am not constrained to make "sex" "from"
"My" own obdurate flesh alone.
"I also" "have"
Opportunities "to make sex"
Out "of words" "and"

Concepts. Therefore, "as" "a poet"
Even "I might" be considered
"Sexy." "The" ingredients "of"
"My" "being" "are"
"Words" "and" "flesh" "mostly." "Everyone"
Has "the" same "flesh"

Only "the" "words" "are" different.
"A" recovered "name" suddenly
Floods "the" memory "taken from
The shop where I
Was made." "I" once gave someone "a"
Dictionary.

~~~~~~

Some of these poems first appeared in *6 × 6, 1913: A Journal of Forms, Area Sneaks, Called Back Sampler, Colorado Review, Critical Quarterly, Effing, Fence, Lana Turner, LIT, The Nation, No: A Journal of the Arts, Out of Nothing, Realpoetik, The Sienese Shredder,* and *Triple Canopy.* Two groups of poems were collected in chapbooks: *Cold Genius* (The Physiocrats, 2009), and *Four Mottoes of Exchange* (The Song Cave, 2014).

Thanks are due to the editors, and to Jalal Toufic, Jean-Baptiste Joly, Silke Pflüger, and the staff and fellows at Akademie Schloss Solitude, where this book was completed.

Published in the United States by Fence Books
Science Library 320
University at Albany
1400 Washington Ave.
Albany, NY 12222

Design: Mark Owens
Printing in Canada by The Prolific Group

Fence Books are distributed by University Press of New England
www.upne.com

Library of Congress Cataloguing-in-Publication Data
Kunin, Aaron [1973–]
Cold Genius: A Book of Poems/ Aaron Kunin
Library of Congress Control Number: 2014945616

ISBN: 978-1-934200-84-1

FIRST EDITION
10 9 8 7 6   5 4 3 2